Niizh

ALSO BY JOELLE PETERS

Frozen River (nîkwatin sîpiy)
(with Michaela Washburn and Carrie Costello)

Niizh

JOELLE PETERS

PLAYWRIGHTS CANADA PRESS

Toronto

First edition: October 2024
Printed and bound in Canada by Imprimerie Gauvin Ltée, Gatineau

Jacket art and design by Chief Lady Bird and provided courtesy of Native Earth Performing Arts
Author photo © Gaetz Photography

Playwrights Canada Press
202-269 Richmond St. W., Toronto, ON M5V 1X1
416.703.0013 | info@playwrightscanada.com | www.playwrightscanada.com

LIBRARY AND ARCHIVES CANADA CATALOGUING IN PUBLICATION
Title: Niizh / Joelle Peters.
Names: Peters, Joelle, author.
Identifiers: Canadiana (print) 20240422341 | Canadiana (ebook) 20240422368 | ISBN 9780369105219 (softcover) | ISBN 9780369105226 (PDF) | ISBN 9780369105233 (EPUB)
Subjects: LCGFT: Drama.
Classification: LCC PS8631.E82165 N55 2024 | DDC C812/.6—dc23

Playwrights Canada Press staff work across Turtle Island, on Treaty 7, Treaty 13, and Treaty 20 territories, which are the current and ancestral homes of the Anishinaabe Nations (Ojibwe / Chippewa, Odawa, Potawatomi, Algonquin, Saulteaux, Nipissing, and Mississauga / Michi Saagiig), the Blackfoot Confederacy (Kainai, Piikani, and Siksika), néhiyaw, Sioux, Stoney Nakoda, Tsuut'ina, Wendat, and members of the Haudenosaunee Confederacy (Mohawk, Oneida, Onondaga, Cayuga, Seneca, and Tuscarora), as well as Metis and Inuit peoples. It always was and always will be Indigenous land.

We acknowledge the financial support of the Canada Council for the Arts, the Ontario Arts Council (OAC), Ontario Creates, the Government of Ontario, and the Government of Canada for our publishing activities.

Canada Council for the Arts | Conseil des arts du Canada
ONTARIO ARTS COUNCIL
CONSEIL DES ARTS DE L'ONTARIO
an Ontario government agency
un organisme du gouvernement de l'Ontario
ONTARIO CREATES | ONTARIO CRÉATIF
Canada
Ontario

This play began as a way for me to bring my voice to the world of romantic comedies.

I needed to see people that looked like me, that spoke like me, that grew up in a community like mine, fall in love. As the development continued, I discovered that the world of *Niizh* was far more expansive than I first imagined. It's a world that is deeply rooted in the love of land, of family, and of self.

I dedicate *Niizh* to the Indigenous youth trying to find their place in the world. I hope you see yourself in this story, and that it inspires you to carve out your own path . . . you can do anything you set your mind to.

Chi-miigwetch.

FOREWORD

Eva Thomas

Joelle Peters brings to life a heartfelt and humorous narrative in *Niizh*, set in a reserve in southwestern Ontario. This coming-of-age tale centres around Lenna Little, the youngest member of the Little family, as she prepares to embark on her journey to university. Along the way, she encounters Sam Thomas, a young man returning to the reserve after a prolonged absence. Through their encounter, Joelle skilfully crafts a narrative that celebrates Indigenous identity, language, family dynamics, and the tender blossoming of young love.

Niizh—"two" in Anishinaabemowin—aptly reflects Lenna's internal struggle of balancing between the pursuit of her dreams and the pull to remain rooted close to home, a conflict resonant with many Indigenous people when leaving their communities. Throughout the play, Lenna finds the courage to confront and navigate these conflicting desires, ultimately discovering that her identity and aspirations are not mutually exclusive from her roots and community. She learns to embrace both aspects of herself, finding strength in her cultural heritage while pursuing her aspirations beyond her familiar surroundings. In doing so, Lenna's journey becomes a poignant reflection of resilience, self-discovery, and the intricate layers of Indigenous identity.

My connection to Joelle and this play runs deep. We both come from the same community: Walpole Island First Nation (Bkejwanong Territory), and I had the privilege of teaching Joelle in the very first acting class I conducted for youth on our reserve. From the start, Joelle was a charismatic and passionate student, eager to learn about acting, auditions, scene work, commercials, and modelling. After our program, there was an opportunity to audition for a local production of *Peter Pan*, and Joelle, seizing the moment, secured the role of Tiger Lily. Seeing her now, many years later, as a professional actor and writer fills me with immense joy. And I like to think that I had a small part in encouraging her interest in acting and performing.

When the play premiered in Toronto, I was asked to facilitate the Q&A after both the opening night and the performance attended by youth from our community who rode a bus into the city from the rez. It was powerful to see my community represented on stage. I recognized the people, the land, the language, and even the local radio station. Seeing my community represented was such a lovely experience. I know the youth from the community also enjoyed the performance. There is real power in representation and seeing yourself in stories.

As someone who has witnessed Joelle's journey from a passionate young student to a professional artist and leader, I am incredibly proud of her achievements. Her role as Artistic Director of Native Earth Performing Arts and her recognition as the Siminovitch Prize protegée for playwriting by laureate Tara Beagan stand as proof of her talent and dedication.

Niizh is a celebration of Indigenous identity and language. Recognizing the potential to integrate Anishinaabemowin into the script, Joelle collaborated closely with a language keeper from our community, skilfully interweaving meaningful Anishinaabemowin into the play. This inclusion adds depth and authenticity to the narrative, underscoring the richness of the play's portrayal of Indigenous identity and culture.

The play emerges as a significant contribution to Indigenous representation in Canadian theatre. Joelle's dedication to depicting Indigenous characters in all their complexity—flawed, funny, loving, and real—challenges stereotypes and offers a fresh perspective on Indigenous experiences. This play serves as an important step toward greater authenticity and diversity in storytelling, providing a platform for Indigenous voices to be heard and celebrated. It invites audiences on a journey infused with humour and love, a testament to Joelle's remarkable talent. I am honored to be part of Joelle's journey and to witness the impact of her work on our community and beyond.

Chi-miigwech, Joelle, for bringing our stories to life with such grace. And I am very excited to see what you do next!

Eva Thomas is a writer, director, and producer. She has directed episodes of CBC*'s* Still Standing *and written for* Zarqa, Shelved, Acting Good, *and* Don't Even. *Her short film,* Redlights, *premiered at the Toronto International Film Festival (*TIFF*) and is being developed into a feature film. She was Associate Producer on the feature film* Night Raiders, *directed by Danis Goulet. Eva has participated in prestigious industry programs like the* BIPOC *Showrunner Bootcamp, Women in the Director's Chair, and* TIFF *Filmmakers Lab. Eva is a member of Walpole Island First Nation and is dedicated to diverse storytelling and mentorship.*

Niizh was commissioned by the Blyth Festival and received developmental support through Native Earth Performing Arts's Animikiig Creator's Unit. It was first produced by Native Earth Performing Arts at the Aki Studio, Toronto, from April 12–30, 2023, with the following cast and creative team:

Lenna: Theresa Cutknife
Sam: Kole Durnford
Jay: Aren Okemaysim
Dad/Billy: Jason McDonald
KC/Bird: PJ Prudat

Director: desirée leverenz
Production Manager and Technical Director: Julia Howman
Stage Manager: Jessica Campbell-Maracle
Assistant Stage Manager: Dylan Tate-Howarth
Set Designer: Nancy Perrin
Head of Props: Sarah Yuen
Props Assistant: Aden Altamirano
Lighting and Projections Designer: Hailey Verbonac
Sound Designer: Jenna Geen
Costume Designer: Nishina Loft
Costume Design Assistant: Halle Turner
Language Consultant: Mko Giizoons
Choreography Consultant: Aria Evans
Fight Director: Richard Comeau

CHARACTERS

Lenna Little (pronounced Len-nah): Jay's sister, Billy's daughter. Used to work part-time with her dad at the convenience store on the reserve. Leaving for college soon.

Sam Thomas: Son of "Jazz" Thomas (Jazz is not seen in the play), KC's nephew. Student at the University of Windsor (UWin, Business). Lives with his mom in Windsor.

Jay Little: Lenna's brother, a few years older than her. Billy's son. Sometimes works at a local farm. Friends with Kenny G and Alpha (not seen in the play). Used to work at Billy's store till he broke the cash register. Fractured relationship with Billy.

Dad/Billy Little: Lenna and Jay's dad. Friends and neighbours with KC. Owns a local business, Billy's General Store, on the reserve. Hard-working with side of dad jokes. Recovering from a heart-related health issue. Pepsi, not Coke.

KC: Looks out for Lenna and Jay like an auntie would, used to babysit them when they were younger. Sam's actual auntie. Friends and neighbours with Billy. Jazz's sister. Easygoing and fiercely loyal to her loved ones.

Radio DJ: Voice-over by the actor that plays Dad/Billy, or separately recorded by someone else entirely. Player's choice. It should not sound like Billy works at the radio station.

Bird: Performed by the actor that plays KC. Projections or puppetry represent her just fine. Probably small in size, but big in spirit.

SETTING

A reserve in Southwestern Ontario.

NOTE

A forward slash (/) indicates the point at which the character that speaks next interrupts the character that is currently speaking.

Pre-show sounds: Rez radio. Old-timey country, bluegrass, classic rock, rural/small-town vibes. Nothing too current or hip. In between songs, there's a recording of an Anishinaabemowin lesson, sharing word translations from Ojibwe to English. Please consult the playwright to discuss this if unclear.

This is a place that a land acknowledgement could go.

For the world premiere, in discussion with the playwright, director, and cast, it was decided that the play itself is a land acknowledgement and so an "official" land acknowledgement was foregone. However, should it feel appropriate for the cast or theatre presenting a new production (especially if presented at a non-Indigenous theatre company), it could go something like this:

The voices of the actors share their names and the traditional lands they're from. Maybe they start to slowly overlap and grow until they come together to acknowledge the lands that everyone is currently gathered on.

Static again. And then a rez radio station:

RADIO DJ: *(voice-over)* You're listening to 98.3 CFRZ "The Cruise." Chiiiii-miigwetch for joining us today, cousins. I hope you're having a good one, wherever you're tuning in from. Just a couple community reminders: if you're planning on heading down to Billy's General Store please note he's off tomorrow morning for a doctor's appointment, the door will be locked, and lights will be off till about hiiigh noon. Maybe later, if he stops somewhere for lunch. Ehhhh, just kiddin'.

And hey, now that summer's here garbage pickup gets pushed back an hour, so make sure you don't put your trash bags out too soon. Gotta time it juuust right or them rez dogs will be having a feast.

Well, I think that about covers it for now. Give me a call here at the station if you've got any other notices or even song requests . . . hey, any birthdays out there? The number here is—

Static.

Sounds of nature.

PROLOGUE

Soundscape: nature (frogs croaking, crickets chirping, birds singing, water nearby).

It is semi-dark and we are in a place that feels both familiar and strange, like a dream.

LENNA *enters and the world awakens. She goes to a tree stump and sits on it, looking out at the sky, her surroundings. She picks a couple of weeds and touches the ground.*

It is an early summer morning.

LENNA: I'm leaving soon, Misho. Just a few more weeks. I'm going off to school, like you wanted. Like I want to. Need to.

Can you see, Misho? I've taken care of our spot. Just like you asked me to. I never missed a Sunday evening visit. The wildflowers still grow here, those little yellow ones you used to bring over to the house sometimes. "Waawaaskone" you'd say, holding them out for me. The language always seemed to come back to you when we visited out here. And the flowers always smelled better than store-bought ones.

Beat.

I dunno what to do with . . . this.

I'm leaving soon, Misho. Just a couple more weeks.

I wish you were still here. I wish I could hear you say how proud of me you are.

I hope I never forget this place. Even more, I hope that it never forgets me.

She exits.

SCENE 1

Lights come up to reveal a rez house—the Little family home. There's some wood paneling in the hallway but it's been removed everywhere else. We see the kitchen and living room. The audience can see people as they walk up the gravel driveway and as they leave. JAY *Little approaches the house carrying a small pile of mail. He enters, throws the pile of papers onto the kitchen table, and continues to the living room, grabbing the remote and flipping channels on the* TV *until he finds a baseball game. He sits and watches.*

LENNA *enters, kicks her shoes off at the door, and she and her brother give each other the nod. She disappears down the hall.* JAY *gets up, returns to the table, and starts sorting through the mail when he comes across three neon-coloured flyers.*

JAY: Ya gotta be kidding me!

LENNA: *(off stage)* Huh?

JAY: Remember the other day when I was telling Kenny G to hold off on having a taco sale?
That little punk didn't listen to me. He's having one tomorrow!

LENNA *doesn't respond. She re-enters carrying her bag and is immediately ambushed.*

Here, take a look at this.

JAY *holds out the other two neon-coloured flyers for her.*

LENNA: Kelly's having a taco sale.

JAY: Now look at the other flyer.

LENNA: . . . and Marv too.

JAY: And all three of 'em are . . .

LENNA: Tom/orrow.

JAY: / Tomorrow! I can't believe this.

LENNA: What's the big deal?

JAY: There's an unspoken rule around NDN taco sales: no more than two sales in one day.

LENNA: What's wrong with three taco sales?

JAY: Two's a party, three's a crowd. Everybody knows that.

LENNA: Not Kenny G.

JAY: *(thinking)* This must be why he asked to hang out tomorrow. "Swing by around ten." Nuh-uh. Nope. Not doing that.
And did you see how much he's charging? Ten bucks? Guy's out of his mind. No one's gonna buy that.

LENNA: I didn't know you were so invested in NDN taco etiquette.

JAY: I remember when everybody sold 'em for like six bucks. And that included a pop.

LENNA: The times are changing. People gotta live. Stuff costs more now.

> *JAY rolls his eyes, grumbling. LENNA clocks the time and starts making a sandwich. She tosses it in her bag.*

Remember when dad used to make frybread?

JAY: His was the best.

DAD walks in.

DAD: Who's the best?

He does a bodybuilding pose. JAY shakes his head and exits silently.

LENNA: We were talking about your frybread.

DAD: It was award-winning. Legendary.

LENNA: So legendary your doctor said you shouldn't be making it anymore.

DAD: Yeah, yeah. What does that guy know?

LENNA: I'd guess a fair amount.

DAD: An NDN without frybread is like a guitar with no strings.

LENNA: Uh . . .

DAD: A year without rain.

LENNA: Dad.

DAD: A fish without water!

LENNA: Oh my god you're so dramatic.

DAD: Hey, KC gave me some totes earlier. Said they're for you. They're in the back of the truck if you wanna get them before I head out.

LENNA: Okay.

DAD: When you leaving again?

LENNA: The date's been on the calendar since May.

DAD: And what's that date again?

LENNA: August 20th.

DAD: I thought school didn't start till fall.

LENNA: Yeah, but I wanna get settled in my dorm before classes start, and there's this whole orientation week where they show you around and stuff.

> *DAD starts looking through the pile of mail JAY brought in. He sees the three taco sales, raises an eyebrow but says nothing.*

Did you think about whether you wanna come up to drop me off or not?

DAD: I'll probably be busy at the store. Been a little short-staffed since you left.

LENNA: I put that "Help Wanted" sign in the window a while ago, nobody reached out?

DAD: They did. But I've been too busy for new hires. Training takes too long.

> *LENNA frowns. DAD checks the time.*

Hey, you wanna come by the shop later? I could use your help with stocking. Shipment gets in around five.

LENNA: I gotta head into town for some errands.

DAD: C'mon, it won't take long. And Barbie wants to see ya too.

LENNA: . . . yeah I guess.

DAD: Thanks. Hey, make me a sandwich? I gotta head out.

LENNA: So do I.

DAD: I don't have time, c'mon Lenna.

LENNA: Then you should've made time.

DAD: Quit being lippy and do it. Hurry up.

DAD storms out of the room and heads down the hall.

LENNA is still for a moment then gets up and throws together a peanut butter and jam sandwich. She puts it in a sandwich bag and leaves it on the table, tossing the knife into the sink.

SCENE 2

Outside the Little house. A car pulls up, shuts off, and LENNA *walks up the driveway, struggling with groceries.*

KC: *(off stage)* Hi-di-ho, neighbour!

KC *walks over from her house next door.*

LENNA: *(still struggling with groceries)* Hey KC.

KC: Need a hand?

Before LENNA *answers she grabs a couple of the bags.* LENNA *reaches for her house keys.*

LENNA: Thanks.

KC: Miigwetch.

LENNA: Miigwetch.

LENNA *gets the door open and they head inside, setting the groceries down on the counter and table.*

KC: What's on the menu tonight?

LENNA: Jay wants potato salad and grilled burgers—

LENNA *realizes.*

Shit, I forgot to get propane earlier.

KC: You're welcome to use my BBQ if you want. I got myself a hot date tonight, so I won't be around.

Remember that guy I talked about meeting at karaoke in town a couple weeks ago?
Finally decided to give him a ring. We're gonna go see a movie.

LENNA: Pretty soon he'll be giving you a ring.

KC: Holy, settle down.

LENNA: That'll be you and him.

KC: What is this, a rom-com?

LENNA: Can I be your maid of honour at the wedding?

KC: Knock it off! . . . and obviously!

They laugh, KC *shoves* LENNA*'s arm.* LENNA *looks at the time.*

LENNA: Ugh, I better head out. Dad wants me to help him with new stock at the store.

KC: Jeez that guy. He knows you don't work there anymore, right?

LENNA: Doctor says he shouldn't be lifting too much so he needs help.

KC: Where's Jay?

LENNA: Jay's still banned from the store. Last time he worked he broke the register and it took forever to get it fixed. So it's just easier if I do it.

KC: How's your dad gonna survive after you leave?

LENNA: We almost had a conversation about it earlier. He actually asked when I'm leaving. I was amazed. He shut it down pretty quick though, went back to being pissed that I'm making things more difficult for him.

KC: You're his little girl, getting ready to leave the nest for the first time ever. First generation to go to college. It's a big deal.

LENNA: Dad doesn't care about any of that. All he talks about is how much work there is to do. And I know he's never gonna hire someone to help out at the store. He's too stubborn. He's probably hoping I drop out before the end of first semester so I can come back to work and he can gloat.

KC: Hey. I know that isn't true. And it isn't your job to worry about all that stuff.

LENNA: I guess.

KC: Trust me, my girl. You're gonna have a good time out there. It's fun, making your own decisions. You wanna eat microwave popcorn for dinner? Go for it, your choice. You wanna stay up till 2 a.m.? Who's gonna get after you? Nobody. You wanna skip class? Well, you better not, because you're there to get an education.
You're finally gonna be able to focus on yourself and your future, instead of having to take care of your dad and Jay all the time. You are not a caretaker. You hear me?

LENNA: I don't know how to just focus on me. It's never been like that.

KC: You'll figure it out. And if you get into trouble, you call me. Okay? I'll head up there anytime you need me. I'm so excited for you, kiddo.

LENNA: Thanks, KC.

KC: Miiiigwetch.

LENNA: Miigwetch. Right.

KC: Well, I'm gonna head out. Spare key for my place is in its usual spot, don't forget to put it back when you're done.

LENNA: Thanks again. Miigwetch. I mean. Again.

KC exits.

(shouting out the door) Good luck on your date!

SCENE 2A

The dream world. LENNA *is in a field alone. She feels calm, peaceful. It is a safe place for her. A bird lands on a nearby tree branch and whistles a tune.* LENNA *whistles back. The two sing to each other and it feels like a conversation with an old friend. Suddenly, the sky grows dark.* LENNA *looks up at the sky, and it begins to rain.*

BIRD: *(in Ojibwe)* Why are you crying?

LENNA: *(in Ojibwe)* I'm not crying, it's raining.

BIRD: *(in Ojibwe)* Oh. Am I crying?

LENNA: *(in Ojibwe)* I can't tell.

BIRD: *(in Ojibwe)* I'm going to look for worms now. Can you see yourself out?

LENNA: Yes.

The BIRD *flies away.* LENNA *stands, maybe not quite sure how she got there after all. She thinks for a moment and then exits.*

SCENE 3

A car pulls in the driveway. The car door opens and shuts, and someone walks through gravel. We see SAM *Thomas carrying a stuffed duffle bag, two iced coffees, and a few reusable bags full of groceries as he walks toward the Little house. He pulls out his phone, looks down at it, at the house, at his phone, at the house, then puts it away. He seems nervous. He makes his way to the front door and stops, staring at it. Hesitation. Then, he swings the front door open and takes a step inside.*

He's unsure now, but he sets his bags down regardless.

He goes to the fridge and starts to put things away. LENNA *enters from the hallway—*SAM *doesn't hear or see her yet.*

LENNA: . . . Can I help you?

SAM *jumps, startled. The grocery bags slip out of his hand and fall, the contents spill out on the floor. Like a deer that perhaps found themselves somewhere they shouldn't be, he fumbles around awkwardly.*

Sorry, didn't mean to scare you. Here, let me help you—

They both go to pick up some things, getting in each other's way. SAM *accidentally elbows* LENNA *in the face as he bends to grab a bag. She steps away, grabbing her nose.*

SAM: Shit! I'm so sorry! Are you okay?!

LENNA: Y-yeah I'm good.

She moves her hand from her face, and they look at each other for the first time. His eyes widen.

. . . what?

SAM: Blood. Bleed. Your . . .

LENNA: *(touching her nostril, realizing)* Oh. Yeah. That's happening.

She tilts her head upward.

SAM: Just a bit though! It's not bad. I don't know. Is it? You're okay. Unless it hurts. Does it hurt? Is your nose broken? I'm so sorry. Here, I'll grab a paper towel or something. I think I have one in my bag. Just hold on!!

LENNA: No! I'm fine, I can just go /

SAM: / Holy shit. Did I head-butt you? It all happened so fast—

He digs in his bag and finds tissues.

Here ya go. Sorry, these are all crumpled. I didn't use them . . . man. They look gross, don't they? You don't have to use them if you don't want to . . . they've been in there for a while. I just keep 'em for emergencies like this—

LENNA: No, don't worry about it! No harm done. It's not like I lost an eye or anything.

SAM: Could you imagine? You'd have to wear an eye patch, and I don't have one of those. Whew. Are you okay? Do you need to sit down?

LENNA: Yes. No. I can stand. I'm good. Thanks.

Beat.

SAM: Sorry. But who are you?

LENNA: I feel like I should be the one asking you that.

SAM: Huh?

LENNA: This is my house.

SAM: This is your . . . oh. No. Wait. This is KC's house.

LENNA: No, it's my house. KC's over there.

She points next door.

SAM: Ah. Oops.

LENNA: It's fine, it happens.

SAM: Ah, cool. Cool cool cool.

SAM stands, shifting his weight.

LENNA: So . . . who are you?

SAM: Oh yeah. Howdy. I'm Sam.

LENNA: Lenna. Nice to meet you.

SAM: Lenna, hey. Yeah I'm KC's nephew.

LENNA: Nephew?

SAM: Yeah.

LENNA: I didn't know KC had a nephew.

SAM: Yep, sure does. Nice to meet you.

SAM extends his hand.

LENNA: You . . . too.

LENNA awkwardly shakes his hand.

SAM: I'm here to see Auntie KC. Do you know if she's around?

LENNA: I think she's at work.

SAM: Oh yeah, the library right? Maybe I'll head that way.

LENNA: Did she know you were coming?

SAM: Yeah. Or no, not really, but we were chatting and she said I could come visit anytime. I used to live here—not here, of course, but like around here. Anyway that was . . . it's been a while.

LENNA: Uh, welcome back then. I can go give her a call. We don't really get cell service out here so I gotta use the landline. Two seconds. Or, can I get you something? Water? We might have some juice boxes . . . ?

SAM: Sure, I could go for some grape juice.

LENNA: Sorry, we only have apple. I should've specified—

SAM: Oh. No, I'm good then. Or, I can—never mind. I'm good.

LENNA: Are you sure?

SAM: Yeah. No. Sorry.

LENNA: You're not good?

SAM: No, I meant

LENNA: Here, just take one.

LENNA tosses the juice box in SAM's direction. He misses. It clunks on the floor.

Shit. My bad.

She grabs the house phone and walks outside to the front step, dialing a number. Waits. Voicemail. While she's on the phone, SAM looks around the house a bit. He takes a closer look at the NDN taco flyers. While she's outside, SAM begins stretching.

LENNA: *(on phone)* Hey KC, it's Lenna. Umm . . . you got a visitor, or I guess, I've got a visitor . . . for you? He says he's your nephew. But I didn't even know you had a nephew . . . so . . . yeah. He's here. And I'm here. He's got short brown hair, brown eyes . . . uh . . . wearing a white shirt. Looks like he ironed it. He seems nice enough . . . but still, kinda weird you never told me you had a nephew so I'm a little sketched out and . . . well. Uh. Okay. Well. Just letting you know. He's here. At my house. With me. Call me back please. K. Bye. Baamaapii.

She walks back inside. SAM is mid-lunge.

LENNA: Left her a voicemail.

SAM: Great, thank you so much.

Beat. A rez dog barks in the distance.

(stretching) Man. I slept weird last night. Should've stretched before making the drive from Windsor.

LENNA: You came from Windsor?

SAM: I live there, me and my mom.

LENNA: Oh cool. She didn't come with you?

SAM: No, just me. She didn't wanna come.

He quickly changes the subject.

Yeah. I go to UWin, just finished my first year. Supposed to go back soon, but I don't know.

LENNA: Don't know what?

SAM: If I want to go. To school. Doesn't feel right.

LENNA: Doesn't feel right.

LENNA sits at the table and gestures for SAM to join her. He does.

SAM: I know this is gonna sound weird, but I started having these dreams? About this place.

LENNA: My house?

SAM: Sorry. Not this place, I mean the rez. I haven't been back since I was a kid.

LENNA: What were the dreams about?

SAM: It's gonna sound weird so try not to judge me too hard. But it was about being on the land. Hearing the birds, the wind in the trees. Frogs croaking. My grandma's backyard. A bonfire. That tiny stream by the band office.

LENNA: I think that dried up a few years ago.

SAM: Damn, RIP stream. Well, I've been pretty disconnected from myself, my teachings, my family, community, whatever, for a long time.

When I started having the dreams, I reached out to KC and she invited me out, so. Here I am.

LENNA: You just up and left? Because of some dream about the dried-up stream by the band office?

SAM: It was more than that. But I know. It sounds dumb.

LENNA: No, it's not. Sorry. Just most people I know around here are dying to leave, not come back.

SAM: Are you dying to leave?

LENNA: I dunno if I'd say that, but I'm leaving for school soon. Starting at Sheridan in a couple weeks.

SAM: Congrats. Which program?

LENNA: General arts. Not really sure what I wanna do yet. Just . . . time to get out of here.

SAM: I'm in business. Not really sure I wanna stick with it though. My high school guidance counsellor said it was either that or go into the trades.

LENNA: Mine told me I should go into nursing. Or something with kids. But I don't like either of those.

Beat.

SAM: You guys close with KC?

LENNA: She used to babysit me and my brother Jay when we were younger. My misho babysat us during the week, and KC took weekends when my dad worked early. KC made the best chocolate chip pancakes.

SAM: I remember those! She made them for me once.
Did your mom work a lot too?

LENNA: I dunno. Her and my dad are divorced.

SAM: Oh. I'm sorry.

LENNA: It's okay. She left when I was like five. I don't really remember her.

SAM: I'm like that with my dad. I don't remember him at all.
I wish I got to spend more time with KC growing up. You were lucky.

LENNA: I guess.

SAM: KC used to come up for visits but her and my mom always ended up fighting about something. Then one day she stopped coming.

LENNA: She was really there for me and my brother growing up, I'm not sure my dad could've raised us without KC or my misho around.

A loud truck rumbles by.

SAM: How's your nose?

LENNA: No more blood, so yay for that.

SAM: I feel awful. I've never hit someone before.

LENNA: Really?

SAM: Have you?

LENNA: Once or twice.

SAM: Oh yeah?

LENNA: Growing up with a brother means the occasional fight, especially when he was really into WWE.

SAM: I don't know why, but that just reminded me of this one time I was down here visiting, and my mom sent me to school with one of my cousins . . . it was recess and I was over by the basketball courts when I saw these two girls arguing. One of them was wearing a turtleneck with a smiling puppy on the front, that's like engrained in my memory. Anyway, she kicked mud at the other girl and it flew all over her coat. Her hair too.

LENNA: . . . what did you just say?

SAM: She had long hair, braided down her back. I remember thinking that would suck to wash all that mud out. Oh! One of them had a WWE backpack. Rey Mysterio was on it. There we go.

LENNA: Oh my god.

SAM: Yeah. Then the girl threw the biggest punch I've ever seen. Hit that girl in the turtleneck right in the face.

LENNA: Sam?

SAM: It's a pretty vivid memory, she cried for a long time. I remember her grandma had to come get her.

LENNA: It wasn't that bad . . .

SAM: Wasn't that bad? Wait, were you there?

LENNA: That was me.

SAM: Smiling puppy?

LENNA: Braided hair. My brother's hand-me-down backpack.

SAM: Holy shit.
Didn't you knock out her two front teeth?

LENNA: Okay, okay, yeah. But she started it! You saw!

SAM: You had a good arm.

A car pulls up, KC steps out and walks over to the Little house.

LENNA: No one else saw the beginning of the fight, they thought I started it. I got detention for a week! And all this time, there was a witness.

KC enters.

KC: Boozhoo! Anishinaa?

SAM: KC!

KC: Hey kiddo, get over here!!

They hug.

What's up with the mess in here?

LENNA: That's Sam's stuff. He dropped it so he could elbow me in the face.

SAM: That's not what happened!

LENNA laughs.

KC: Ahh, Lenna's tough. She popped this girl in the face back in elementary school, took out her two front teeth. Her gram still calls her Bucky to this day . . . who's her mom again? . . . Horse! Good ol' Horse.

SAM: Bucky's mom is named Horse?

LENNA: / Yeah.

KC: / No, well yeah, it's her nickname.

SAM: How'd that happen?

KC: Ohh she probably just liked horses or something. You know how it is. That's how Jazz got her nickname eh.

LENNA: Jazz?

SAM: Yeah, you're right.

KC: That's Sam's mom. Anyway, how goes it? That was quite the voicemail, Lenna . . .

The landline rings. LENNA answers it.

LENNA: *(on the phone)* Hello? . . . what do you want, Jay?
I can't right now. I'm busy.
Go ask Alpha. Or Kenny G.
. . . okay, okay, I'll be there in a couple minutes. Just stay there. Don't make me look for you.

She hangs up.

I've gotta head out and rescue Jay. I'll see you guys later?

SAM: Yeah, definitely.

KC: I might be gone by time you're back, but Sam should be around. Eh, Sam? Yous two can keep getting to know each other.

KC tosses a secret wink in LENNA's direction. LENNA mouths "stop it," embarrassed, and rushes out.

SCENE 3A

The dream world. Four birds sit on a branch. They sing. The wind blows, and they struggle to hold on. The wind sways the branch hard, and the birds scatter frantically. Three of the birds stick together, and one flies away. The wind calms and the birds return to the branch, noticing the fourth has left them. Frantically they cry out for her, but she doesn't return. They try to continue their song, but something has changed. They aren't sure who is leading, and who is following. The three cling close to each other for as long as they can until the wind pushes them all away, hard.

SCENE 4

The Little house. LENNA *unlocks the door and enters,* JAY *stumbles in behind her.*

JAY: Chiiiiii-miiiiiigweeeetch, Lenna! My sister Lenna. Lenna Little. Little LENNA!

He shakes water off like a dog. LENNA *grabs a dish towel and throws it at him.*

LENNA: JAY, you're getting water everywhere! Knock it off!

JAY: What??

LENNA: Just go shower or something. You smell like dirt and beer . . . and . . . Cheetos?

JAY: Man, you're always so moody. Moody Lenna. No wait. Moody Lil' Lenna. No. Lil' Moody Lenna Little.

LENNA *cleans up the dripping water on the floor.*

LENNA: Not moody. I'm annoyed.

JAY: What's your deal? The sun is shinin', the birds are singin', it's a beautiful day in the neighbourhood!

LENNA: I can't always come to your rescue when you lose your keys or get stuck somewhere. This is the third time in two weeks!

JAY: Heyyyy, I didn't lose my keys. I know exactly where they are.

LENNA: Then go get them.

JAY: I can't.

They're at the bottom of the river.

LENNA: *(sighing)* And why are they there, Jay?

JAY crouches on a chair.

JAY: So there was this seagull, eh? I was out walking with Kenny G and Alpha, and that dang bird kept following us, giving us dirty looks. It was like . . . it had the eyes of a dude, like he was a shape-shifter or something. Guy was mocking me. Judging me. Ken saw it too if ya don't believe me! He whipped a Dorito at it, but he missed so I looked around and grabbed the first thing I could find and threw it at him . . . happened to be my house keys. I got him though!

LENNA: What happened to Kenny G's taco sale?

JAY: Changed his mind. Did you hear the part about that seagull though?? I showed him. He flew off after that. So we went and celebrated with a little dip in the river.

LENNA: Right on.

JAY collapses on the couch.

JAY: Holy shit, it feels like we're in one of those salad spinners. Didn't we have one of them?

LENNA: No clue. Get up and go change your clothes. They're still damp. Dad will be pissed if the couch gets wrecked.

JAY: Bossy pants.

LENNA: He'll kick you out.

JAY: Wouldn't be the first time.

LENNA: What?

JAY: I'll just move in with Alpha.

LENNA: There's like twenty people living in that house already.

JAY: Not even. More like eight.

LENNA: You know, you could get your own place if you started saving up.

JAY: *(mocking)* YoU cOuLd gEt yOuR oWn pLaCe iF yOu sTaRtEd sAvInG uP.

LENNA: Annnd that's my cue.

JAY: I'm joooking. Hey. Hey. Heeeey. I'm sorry.

LENNA: I can't talk to you when you're like this. I'm going to my room.

LENNA heads down the hall and slams her bedroom door.

JAY: Fine. Fine! Be that way. Yeah. I'm going to my room too.

JAY stomps down the hall and slams his door. LENNA opens hers again.

LENNA: *(yelling)* And don't forget to throw your clothes in the wash!

LENNA slams her door. JAY opens his.

JAY: BOSSYPANTS.

JAY slams his door.

SCENE 5

A new day. SAM *and* KC *are sitting outside on her front deck. An old bluegrass song is fading out on the small radio perched nearby. A pre-recorded message comes on: "Biintoon toganan: clean your ears. Biin-toon to-ga-nan" and then another song starts up.*

KC: Biintoon toganan. Ha! I'll have to remember that one.

SAM *pulls out a small notepad from his pocket and begins writing.*

SAM: Biintoon . . . toganan. What did that mean again?

KC: Clean your ears. Today's words are all about hygiene. Did your mom end up teaching you any language?

SAM: No, she doesn't remember anything.

KC: That's too bad. Our grandparents used to teach us things when we were little, but that was so long ago now . . . I couldn't tell you what half the words were. It's never too late to try again though, eh?

KC *gets up.*

You want some more coffee?

SAM: I think if I have any more, I'll bleed coffee.

KC: Is that a no?

He extends his coffee mug to her. She goes in to fill it.

SAM: *(louder to* KC *inside)* Does the radio station play anything other than gospel and bluegrass?

KC: *(inside the house)* Ha. Sometimes. Depends on who's playing DJ that day.

Beat.

Oh yeah, radio bingo in a few days. I should pick up some cards.

SAM: Radio bingo? Like, regular bingo . . .

KC: But on the radio, so you play at home.

She returns with the coffee mugs.

SAM: Isn't bingo for like, old people?

KC gasps and slaps SAM's arm.

KC: Absolutely not! Radio bingo unites the community, it's a long-standing tradition. I usually go play next door with the Littles. You should join us.

SAM: Sure, I'll play.

They sit, listening to the radio. Birds chirp happily.

KC: Hey so how's school going? You excited to go back soon?

SAM: Ah. Um. I don't know if I'm going back to school.

KC: Oh? Why not?

SAM: I've been wondering if I should take some time off. I don't know if I really like my program or being in school in general. I'm tired of learning about all that . . . I'm way more interested in this kind of stuff—

He gestures to his notepad.

The things I'm learning here, like Anishinaabemowin, and what the community is like. I wanna learn more about my family. Myself.

KC: Hmm. Well . . . let's keep an eye on that, okay? If you really wanna stay you're more than welcome to, but I know school was always important to your mom. She'd want you to finish your program.

SAM: Yeah. I know.

KC: You don't need to have all the answers right now, Sam. That's okay.

SAM: It just feels like there's this big part of me missing, and I wanna find out what it is. Whenever I tried talking to Mom about it, she just brushed it off, but being here . . . things feel clearer here. My head feels less crowded. And then I find myself getting upset about her keeping me from this.

KC: I understand.

SAM: Kids in school used to call me an apple. I know it's a dumb joke but it always stuck with me because it feels true. I'm disconnected. Too urban. There's so much about me that I don't know.

KC: Being urban isn't a bad thing. But yes, finding yourself is an important journey.

SAM: I can tell people I'm from here, I can show off my status card, but that's not enough. I don't know the first thing about our community. How can I claim something I don't know? All I wanted to do is come here and learn about myself. Why is that so hard? Why doesn't Mom get that?

KC: This place reminds her of her old life, the one she left behind.

SAM: Yeah I guess. But that's the thing, she got to live her life here. She knows this place. She made the choice to leave. I didn't. I don't even know my dad.

Beat.

You knew him, right? What was he like?

KC: What has she told you?

SAM: Nothing. Just that we're better off without him. How'd they even meet?

KC: How does anyone meet around here? They went to school together and hung out at parties.
He's—y'know, I'm not sure anymore.
I don't really see him around.

She pauses.

You look a lot like him.

SAM: Is that a good thing?

KC: Ohh back then your dad was considered one of the best-looking guys on the rez. I remember girls getting all mad at your mom when they got together. All jealous.
Hey, if you're looking for a place to start finding out more about our family, check out the archives at the library sometime. We still gotta sort through them but I've seen your great-grandpa's name pop up a few times. Harry Greenbird. He was one of our community's knowledge keepers.

SAM writes the name in his notepad. LENNA emerges, carrying a small box.

LENNA: I come bearing gifts.

KC: Is that what I think it is?

LENNA: Jay was ranting about frybread again earlier and bet me that I couldn't make any, so I had to prove him wrong. But Dad's gonna be home soon, so we gotta destroy the evidence.

SAM: Wow, I haven't had one of these in forever.

LENNA *hands him a piece wrapped in paper towel.*

KC: How is Jay? I saw him splashing around in the river the other day.

LENNA: Yeah. Something about a sketchy seagull.

KC: Sounds about right.

SAM: *(writing in his notepad)* Sketchy . . . seagulls.

SCENE 6

A new day. The Little house. A country song plays on a radio. DAD is at the table fiddling with some fishing line, a tackle box on the table next to him. JAY walks in—he wasn't expecting to see DAD. The two look at each other, a bit of a stare-off, and then JAY gives him the nod. DAD nods back, then goes back to his fishing line. JAY heads to the fridge, grabs a beer, and heads outside. LENNA passes him as she comes in.

DAD: Heya.

LENNA: Hey. Oh, those magazines you wanted came in the mail today.

DAD: The fishing ones?

LENNA: Yeah, I forgot to grab them though. They're still in the car.

DAD: Better go get 'em.

LENNA: I will in a bit.

DAD: Could do it now.

LENNA: Do you need them now?

DAD: No, I'm busy.

LENNA: Then you can wait.

DAD: I didn't raise you to talk back to me. Show some respect.

LENNA goes out to her car and gets the magazines. She throws them on the table.

You wanna try that again?

She picks them up and places them down nicely.

There. Was that so hard?

She doesn't answer him.

Hello?

LENNA: No, it wasn't.

DAD: Hey, what's that new guy like? Jazzie's boy.

LENNA: Do you mean Sam?

DAD: Sammy. Yeah. What's he like?

LENNA: He's fine.

DAD: Ohhh is he?

LENNA: Not like that.

DAD: Hey, you wanna go out in the boat? Tarzan said the perch are biting out in the bay. Even got a couple'a bass.

LENNA: I was thinking about going into town.

DAD: C'mon, you can do that later. The fish are biting now!

LENNA: I don't want to go out in the boat today, Dad.

DAD: Fine.
Well I'll be back around seven, we can eat then. Since you're going to town, you wanna grab something at the store?

LENNA: K.

DAD: I threw some laundry in the machine earlier, should be almost done. You wanna toss it in the dryer?

LENNA: Okay.

DAD: Oh, and another big shipment is coming into the store on Tuesday. Can you throw that in your busy schedule? It's an early one, so show up around eight.

LENNA: You got it.

> *DAD grabs his fishing stuff and heads out. LENNA looks at the messy kitchen table and starts to clean up. The washer sings its "wash done" song. LENNA sighs heavily and collapses at the table, head in her hands. She shoves the tackle box off the side of the table, and it crashes to the floor as JAY enters.*

JAY: What'd that tackle box do to you?

LENNA: It was an accident.

JAY: Yeah. And it had nothing to do with Dad storming outta here?

LENNA: No. Everything's fine.

JAY: Doesn't seem fine, you're throwing tackle boxes around like the Hulk.

LENNA: It just . . . ugh. It's always something. Clean up the table. Wash the dishes. Fold the laundry. Go to the store. Make lunch. Cook dinner. Don't complain. Don't talk back. Be perfect. He's always throwing more stuff on my plate. It's too much.

> *JAY picks up the tackle box and kisses it better, then starts putting some of the fishing things away.*

What if I flunk out?

JAY: Of school?

LENNA: Yeah.

JAY: The school you haven't gone to yet?

LENNA: That's the one.

JAY: In the city you aren't in?

LENNA: Yup.

JAY: You won't.

LENNA: But what if?? I've never done any of this. You, Dad, Misho—none of you went to college. I don't know what I'm doing. I feel ridiculous.

JAY: You're just nervous.

LENNA: It's more than that. I'm gonna fail. I'm gonna flunk. I know it.

JAY: Then you'll try again. Littles don't quit.

LENNA: Mom did.

JAY: Not the same thing.
Nah. You can whine, but you're gonna get up and keep going.

He goes to the sink and starts washing a plate, and then a mug.

LENNA: When did you become the one to give me pep talks?

JAY: What's today?

LENNA: August 2.

JAY: August 2 then.

LENNA puts her head down on the table. JAY finishes up the dish he was washing and heads down the hall.

Lights shift.

SCENE 6A

The dream world.

LENNA wakes up at the table. SAM enters.

SAM: Hey, there you are.

He goes to LENNA and gives her a quick hug and kiss on the cheek.

LENNA: Sorry, was I supposed to meet you somewhere?

SAM: I dunno. You want some tea?

LENNA: Can I make coffee instead?

SAM: I want tea.

LENNA: Okay.

SAM pours water into two mugs and tosses a tea bag in each. He hands one to LENNA and sits in the chair next to her.

SAM: Black, right?

LENNA: You remembered.

She gets up and goes over to the coffee maker. She opens the top and goes to grab the tin of ground coffee. The radio pops on and begins playing a jazz tune. SAM gets up and goes to LENNA, extending his arm to her. She accepts it and they begin to slow dance. He spins her, and she goes to put coffee grounds in the machine and hits start, then returns to the dance.

As the song comes to an end, the lights lower and spotlight the two. They move toward the couch.

Lights shift. SAM *moves in closer to* LENNA *and they are locked in an embrace. We're left with the sounds of a bubbling coffee machine. Something is brewing.*

SCENE 7

A new day at the Little house. Tuesday, to be exact. LENNA *wakes up on the couch. She looks at the time—she's late to meet her dad at the store. She sprints down the hall to change, re-emerging with a toothbrush hanging out of her mouth. She spits in the kitchen sink and throws on her shoes, rushing out the door. We hear a car trying to turn over with no luck, a pause, then another failed attempt. The car door creaks open then slams, and* LENNA *rushes back toward the house. She picks up the landline, dialing. Voicemail.*

LENNA: Shit. Hey! It's Lenna. I slept through my alarm and now my car won't start, I think the battery's dead. I'm gonna keep trying to get a ride, I'll be there soon. Sorry. Bye.

LENNA *disappears somewhere down the hall. We hear someone walking through gravel, and* SAM *appears in the driveway.*

SAM: Lenna?

He knocks on the door. No answer. Suddenly, JAY *appears from out of nowhere behind him.*

JAY: Hey.

SAM: Hey. How's it going?

JAY: Not bad. Beauty day, huh?

SAM: It is. Is Lenna—

JAY: Ohh, Lenna. I see.

JAY *stares at* SAM.

SAM: I was just over at KC's and I saw Lenna having car trouble. So I came over to see if she needs a ride somewhere. I've got a free morning.

JAY: Is that right?

Beat.

C'mon, sit down. Let's chat.

SAM: No, that's—

JAY: Just said you were free all morning, so . . .

SAM sits. He adjusts his shirt, overly conscious of JAY's watchful eye. JAY lights a smoke.

You wanna smoke, Sam?

SAM: N-no, that's okay.

JAY: Why not?

SAM: I don't smoke.

JAY: Ya don't smoke.

SAM: No.

JAY: What, you think you're too good for a smoke?

SAM: No . . .

JAY: Everybody smokes on the rez.

SAM: I kinda have asthma so—

JAY looks at him square in the face. He takes one more long drag of his smoke and then puts it out in the tin can, without looking away from SAM. He squints.

JAY: So . . .

Inside the house, we see LENNA emerge from the hall. She notices the exchange happening outside and scrambles to rush out.

What's your story, huh?

SAM: I—uh . . . what do you wanna know?

LENNA flies out the door.

LENNA: Heeeeey, guys, um, what's up?

JAY: / I was having—

SAM: / I was wondering—sorry.

JAY: No, go ahead.

SAM: I was wondering if you needed a ride somewhere. You looked like you were having car trouble.

JAY: And I was just out for my morning stroll, y'know, getting my steps in.

JAY winks. It's weird.

Y'know I've been hearing the people talking about a new guy around the rez. Word travels fast in these parts, Sam.
So where'd you come from? Who's your mom?

SAM: Windsor.

JAY: Windsor's your mom?

SAM: Me from Windsor. Haha. I mean I'm from Windsor. Well, here. Technically. But I'm just here for the summer. Probably.

JAY & LENNA: Probably?

JAY: Jinx!

LENNA: No one says that anymore.

SAM: Yeah I dunno. I'm staying with KC, and she said I can stay longer if I want to—

LENNA: You're staying?

SAM: I'm not sure yet.

LENNA: You're not going back to school?

JAY: What school?

SAM: UWin. Business.

JAY: Ooh, Sammy the businessman.

SAM: I dunno about that.

JAY: So what do you think of the place so far? People being nice to you around here?

SAM: Y-yeah, everyone's great.

JAY: Anyone tries anything, you come and tell me. I'll take care of 'em.

LENNA: Jay.

JAY: Lenna's got a good arm too. Did she tell you about the time she knocked out some girl's two front teeth?

LENNA: Yes Jay he knows!

JAY: I'm just making sure our new friend knows we've got his back.

SAM: Much appreciated.

JAY: But in order to truly have your back, is there anything I should know? Any skeletons in the closet?

JAY nudges SAM with his elbow a few times.

SAM: Not really . . .

JAY: What's your relationship status? Single?

LENNA: JAY.

SAM: Uhhhhh . . .

LENNA hits JAY with her bag. DAD pulls in the driveway, turns off the truck and walks up with a Pepsi in hand.

JAY: Or you trying to snag?

DAD: Didn't know there was a council meeting in session out here. Hey, is this who I think it is?

LENNA: Yes. Sam, this is my dad. Is that a Pepsi? Dad, it's 8 a.m.

DAD: So?

LENNA: Ugh anyway, we should really get going /

DAD: / Now, now, hold yer horses. Jeeeeez. How's it going, Sam?

DAD pats SAM's back.

JAY: Sammy.

DAD: Spammy? Nah, just kiddin'. How are ya, Sammy? How's your mom?

SAM: Good. We're good.

DAD: Yeah eh. Now what's this I hear about snaggin'?

JAY: That's what we're trying to find out. You snaggin', Salmon?

LENNA: Sammy—no. He is not!! I mean, I don't know—

DAD: Any luck yet, Samuel?

LENNA: Again, guys, it is 8 a.m.

JAY: Snag-o-clock.

SAM: Sorry, I should have asked this earlier but what exactly is "snagging"?

LENNA cringes. JAY pulls out his phone and pushes a button.

JAY: Hey Siri, what is snagging?

His phone beeps and then responds with: "According to Urban Dictionary, 'snagging' is the act of going to a pow wow or First Nations event and hooking up with a girlfriend or boyfriend, or a weekend fling, in reference to fishing when you dip a hook in the water and pull quickly to 'snag' a fish.' Examples include, 'Hey there's a group of hotties, let's go snaggin'' or 'I can't wait to go snaggin' this weekend in Wiki!' By user Tru rez injun."

LENNA covers her face with both hands.

SAM: Cool! Thanks. Uhh, no, I'm not . . . snagging. It looks like you're good here, so I'm just gonna head back over to KC's—

LENNA: *(squeaks)* Great, thanks!

JAY: Guess I know what to tell Princess.

SAM: Who?

LENNA: You don't need to tell Princess anything.

DAD: I thought she was with Blinky.

LENNA: She is.

SAM: Who's the Princess?

JAY: Not anymore. Broke up at Rexy's party.

DAD: Somebody always breaks up at Rexy's parties.

SAM: I'm not really looking to date anybody . . .

DAD: Yeah, you don't need to be somebody's rebound.

JAY: But you could be.

LENNA: We should really get going!

DAD: C'mon, the party's just getting started! You like Pepsi, Sammy? I got another one in the fridge.

JAY: No you don't, I drank it.

DAD: Of course you did. Well, we can share this one Sammy, how's that? Go get us a glass, Lenna—

LENNA: No one needs to be drinking Pepsi at 8 a.m!!!

Silence. A rez dog barks in the distance. LENNA *tries to glare at them without* SAM *seeing.*

SAM: Nice to meet you, Mr. Little.

DAD: Mr. Little?

SAM: Sorry. I don't know your first name—

DAD: I didn't know we were on a first name basis.

SAM *doesn't know how to respond.* DAD *breaks the tension.*

I'm just messin' with ya. Look at him sweat, Lenna!

JAY: Hey, I started those beads of sweat!

LENNA: STOP IT. Go ahead Sam, I'll catch up with you later.

JAY: *(teasing)* Oooooh.

DAD: Wink, wink.

LENNA: SHUT UP!

JAY *tries to wink and shoots finger guns at* SAM, *who quickly escapes with an awkward wave.* LENNA *turns to her dad and brother.*

Can you two relax!? You're so annoying!

JAY: Seems like a decent guy.

DAD: Yeah, I like him.

JAY: Me too. Solid.

LENNA: What?

DAD: Hey, bring him back for dinner. We're having a fish fry! Got lots of fresh perch. We'll eat after radio bingo.

LENNA: He's never gonna wanna come over again.

DAD: He knows we were just jokin' around.

JAY: City NDNS are pretty funny. "Nice to meet you, Mr. Little."

> *JAY moves around robotically, or like the Tin Man from* The Wizard of Oz.

DAD: Real proper that guy. C'mon Lenna, bring him back.

LENNA: I'm sure he has other plans.

DAD: KC's coming over. She already bought extra bingo cards.

JAY: What time's dinner gonna be ready?

DAD: Oh, about snag-thirty.

LENNA: Oh my god. LET'S GO, DAD.

> *She runs off to her dad's truck. JAY and DAD laugh for a moment, then it gets quiet and weird again.*

DAD: You owe me a pop.

> *DAD goes to the truck.*

SCENE 8

Later that day. LENNA *heads over to* KC*'s, the sound of an intense sax solo increases as she gets closer.* SAM *emerges from the house, playing an air sax. He doesn't see* LENNA *yet.*

LENNA: Is this a bad time? Should I come back?

SAM: Ah! Hey. No. KC stepped out so I was just cleaning up.
It's my mom's CD.

LENNA: It's . . . umm . . . nice. I think I've heard it before.

SAM: It's like a comfort thing, I grew up listening to this stuff.

The sax solo intensifies. SAM *turns the volume down.*

. . . Sooooo.

LENNA: Yeah?

SAM: Your family is . . .

LENNA: Sorry about all that earlier.
They like to mess with people. It's all a game to them. The one thing that brings them together.
It's so dumb.

SAM: It's fine!

LENNA: Like every other second of the day they can barely stand to be in the same room together, but find someone to mess with and they're best friends. It's ridiculous.

SAM: They seem nice.

LENNA: They were jerks, you can say that.

SAM: No, I mean it!

LENNA: They're pests. They like you though.

SAM: Yeah?

LENNA: Yep. You're Little approved.

SAM: I'm honoured. Hey, you want some coffee?

LENNA: What?

SAM: I'm gonna throw on a pot of coffee. Or do you want tea?

LENNA: N-no, coffee's fine. Whatever you're having.

He goes to the machine.

Uh. . . do you like fish?

SAM: Not in my coffee.

He pours coffee into a mug and goes to hand it to LENNA. Their hands touch for a second, static. They both jump. The CD skips a beat.

LENNA: Sorry, I think I just shocked you.

They both laugh nervously. Another song comes on.

My dad invited you and KC over for dinner tonight. And for radio bingo. He wants to have like, a fish fry.
I told him you're probably busy, but I figured I'd throw it out there, in case you like . . . fish.

SAM: I'm allergic to shrimp and lobster, but I can do freshwater fish.

LENNA: We don't have either of those, so that's great! Yeah, my dad does a great fish fry. I think you'll like it.

The jazz song gets more jazzy. SAM *turns it down more.*

SAM: I just wanna give my mom a call when she's done work today, but other than that I'm free.

LENNA: How's your mom doing?

SAM: Not sure. She hasn't been answering my calls since I left.

LENNA: Is she okay?

SAM: She is. I had a neighbour check in. She's still upset with me about coming here.
That morning I left, she freaked out, yelling about how there's nothing good for me here.

LENNA: Now that you've seen it for yourself, do you believe her?

SAM: Not at all. I don't see it. She said it was dangerous . . . how's it more dangerous here than in the city?

LENNA: Maybe she didn't mean crime. Maybe she didn't want you digging around in her past.

SAM: But that's the thing, it's not just her past. It's mine too.
I just couldn't shake that feeling, y'know?
Like all semester in school, I'd be sitting in my classes trying to focus on what my profs were saying, and my mind would wander off. I'd start envisioning this place, coming home. Wondering what it'd feel like. One day I even started to see this field? I don't think I've ever actually been there, but it always felt so familiar. Or like a place I'll visit someday.

There was all this long grass surrounding the field. And these tall trees. And when the wind blew, I could smell this sweet, earthy scent. / Sweetgrass.

LENNA: / Sweetgrass.

SAM: And dirt. I haven't smelt sweetgrass in years but it's one of those things your brain never forgets. And I could almost feel the sun on my face. I remember thinking "this is some dream" but it was. . . like more than that. It felt like a memory of something that hasn't happened yet. And I couldn't brush it off. That feeling I got when I went there. I sketched out some of the things I saw—

He pulls out his phone and looks for a photo.

The wildflowers, the tree stumps—see, this is what I saw in my head.

He shows her.

LENNA: You drew this?

SAM: Yeah. It's not very good, I know . . .

LENNA: Sam, you drew a place I know. You're sure you've never been there?

SAM: You know it? Where is it?

LENNA: I—

Beat. She considers.

I can take you there. After dinner. But only if the mosquitoes aren't too bad. And you have to promise that you won't tell anybody else where it is when I show you. Deal?

SAM: After dinner? Won't it be dark then?

LENNA: Not yet. Why? You scared of the dark?

SAM: No, I just . . . we won't really be able to see anything. And aren't there animals out here? Like bears and stuff?

LENNA: No, but I did see a big possum last time. Don't worry, I'll protect you.

LENNA goes to put her hand on his shoulder. SAM smiles at her. She smiles back at him. Suddenly, an intense sax solo interrupts the moment. SAM's eyes widen and he blushes.

SAM: I—I think . . . coffee! I'm gonna get me some of that coffee. Get it while it's hot, eh?

SAM awkwardly gets up and goes inside. LENNA cringes and leaves.

SCENE 9

The Little house. DAD*'s in the kitchen frying fish. Country music plays loudly and he's in his happy place, occasionally singing or dancing a little.* LENNA *walks in the door.*

DAD: Hey, there she is!

LENNA: Holy, are your eyes okay?

LENNA *opens a window and goes to the door, fanning it.*

DAD: Oh, it isn't that bad in here. Try a piece, it's my best batch yet.

He points to a big bowl on the counter.

LENNA: That's a lot of fish. Are you feeding the whole rez?

DAD: Not even. You wanna mix up some coleslaw? Stuff's in the fridge.

LENNA: Sure. I'm just gonna go change first.

DAD: What, you got a special coleslaw outfit?

LENNA: Pff . . . no.

We hear the oil bubbling. LENNA *returns wearing a different shirt and is putting on earrings. She gets the coleslaw stuff from the fridge.*

DAD: Nice earrings.

LENNA: . . . thanks.

DAD: Hey does he play guitar or anything? Maybe we can jam sometime.

LENNA: Who?

DAD: You know who.

LENNA: Oh. I dunno.

DAD: Sure be cool if he did.

LENNA: You'll have to ask him yourself.

The front door swings open.

KC: Ding dong!

DAD: What'd you call me?

KC: Ha.

KC playfully punches his shoulder.

How's it goin'?

DAD: The grease is hot, fish are fried, it's a beautiful day in the neighbourhood.

KC: Brought us some sun tea. Sugar-free, just for you.

DAD: Gross.

KC: You're welcome.

KC grabs a seat at the table.

LENNA: *(glancing out toward KC)* Is Sam on his way?

KC: Nope, just me. Sam's on his way back to Windsor.

LENNA: Like for good?

KC: No, no, just for the night. Something came up.

DAD: Hey, do you know if he plays guitar?

KC: No clue. Are we gonna eat any time soon? I'm starving.

LENNA: I'll get the plates.

LENNA gets up to grab them.

DAD: And here I made all this extra fish for you guys and Sammy bails on us . . .

KC: Oh quit it. I'll bring him leftovers. Or he can come get them himself, eh? Wink wink?

DAD: Wink wink!

LENNA: Hush you two!

Beat, then DAD leans in to whisper to KC.

DAD: Sam's coming back, right?

KC: Far as I know.

DAD: You think if he decides to stick around for good, Lenna might too?

KC slaps his arm.

Hey!

KC: Is that why you're so keen on him?

JAY enters.

JAY: Followed the smell of grease all the way down the road.

KC: Pull up a seat, we're just about to eat.

LENNA starts to dish out the food.

JAY: Where's Samsonite?

DAD: He's not coming.

JAY: Why not? *(turns to LENNA)* What'd you do?

LENNA: I didn't do anything!

KC: He had some family stuff come up.

DAD: All right, somebody say grace.

KC: Grace.

DAD: 'Kay, dig in.

They do.

JAY: Why are you all dressed up?

LENNA: I'm not.

JAY: Never seen you wear earrings before.

DAD: I didn't even know your ears were pierced.

KC: I think they look very nice on you. Are those new?

LENNA: Just thought I'd try something different. Is that so wrong?

JAY shrugs. They eat. LENNA removes her earrings and goes to put them away in her bedroom.

SCENE 9A

Dream world.

JAY lights a few candles and is polishing silverware. He wears a top hat and has an extravagant moustache. DAD appears out of nowhere, also sporting an extravagant moustache. He wears a chef's hat. He's frying a book in a pan on the table. LENNA enters.

DAD: You made it! Please take your seat.

LENNA sits. DAD and JAY grab a tablecloth and start to wave it around. They lift it and, when it drops, SAM appears from behind it. He wears a suit jacket and flip-flops. JAY does a seagull cry. SAM approaches LENNA and kisses her cheek.

SAM: You look amazing.

LENNA: Thanks, so do you.

They sit at the table. KC (sporting the largest moustache of them all) has entered at some point, not sure when. JAY flips his hat over and now it's a cup. DAD goes to get the meal and brings it back to the table, setting the plate (a book) in front of LENNA. It's a cat toy shaped like a fish. It flops around on the plate.

This smells great, Dad. Thank you.

DAD: Anything for my little girl.

They pause for a moment, frozen in time. LENNA looks around.

SAM: Lenna.

LENNA: Sam.

The lights shift. The fish continues flopping as everyone dances out.

SCENE 10

The next morning. LENNA *quietly walks over to* KC*'s with her empty drink pitcher and places it on the porch. She turns to leave when* SAM *spots her and comes out to meet her.*

SAM: Morning!

LENNA *takes a moment then gives him the nod.*

How's it going?

LENNA: Super.

SAM: Yeah?

LENNA: Yup. Here, I was just bringing KC's pitcher back.

SAM: Oh, thanks. I'll go put this in the kitchen. Stay here, I'll be right back.

He disappears inside. LENNA *quickly checks her hair and makes sure it looks okay then returns to looking stoic.* SAM *re-enters.*

Hey, sorry I couldn't come by for dinner last night. I texted you to tell your dad thanks for the leftovers, but I don't think it went through. Or did it?

LENNA: Oh, we've been really busy.

SAM: That was some of the best fried fish I've ever had.

LENNA: *(under her breath)* It's even better fresh.

SAM: What was that?

LENNA: Oh, my phone hasn't been receiving texts lately.

SAM: I see. So how was bingo? Did you win?

SAM sits on the steps. LENNA shakes her head.

That's too bad. But at least it sounds like your night was better than mine. I ended up having to go get my stuff from my mom's place. She kicked me out.

LENNA looks at him.

LENNA: She kicked you out?

SAM: All my stuff was piled up outside the apartment when I got there, and she changed the locks so I couldn't get in.

LENNA: Oh shit. Did you talk to your mom?

SAM: Yeah. She screamed about how I'm making a huge mistake, I'm just gonna get hurt, about how I don't respect her anymore . . . it was awful. I tried to tell her about how great KC has been, how great you and your family have been, and about all the stuff I've been learning, like about the archives . . .

LENNA: You think I'm great?

SAM: That's what you got out of all that?

LENNA: Sorry. That wasn't supposed to come out. Continue.

She sits next to him.

SAM: But she wasn't having any of it. She hates that I'm here. She thinks I'm "choosing a side." And she thinks I'm gonna end up like him. My dad.

LENNA: What happened to your dad?

SAM: She always told me she didn't know anything about him. That when they split, they didn't keep in touch. But that wasn't true.

Beat.

Nope. My dad has a whole new family. Yep. He left me and my mom so he could start over and try again. We weren't good enough for him, I guess.

LENNA: I'm—so sorry, Sam.

SAM: It's not like I spent my whole childhood wondering what happened to him, what he was like, thinking he was this great . . . it's . . . whatever.

Beat.

I didn't even tell her I've been thinking about staying longer. That's a whole other can of worms. It was getting late, so we called it for the night, and I started throwing all my stuff into my car. She helped with a few boxes. And then we agreed we'd talk again when we cooled off.

LENNA: Huh.

SAM: What?

LENNA: Nothing. That's just really healthy communication.

SAM: I guess.

LENNA: And here I was trying to make you feel bad for missing a fish fry . . .

SAM: I really wanted to come. I'm sorry my family's kinda messed up.

LENNA: Your family's messed up? You've seen mine. We're not perfect either.

They don't say anything for a while. Then, SAM *reaches his hand over and puts his on hers.*

SAM: Is this okay?

LENNA: Uh yeah! It is.

SAM: I just wanted to make sure.

LENNA: Thanks for checking.

SAM: It kinda felt like there was a moment yesterday, and that sax solo made it weird.

LENNA: So weird! But it wasn't you. It was the sax.

He squeezes her hand. She smiles.

SAM: So how's the prep going for your move? Have you found out who your roommate is yet?

LENNA: No, but it feels like I should've heard something by now, right? I've been checking my email constantly.

SAM: Well when did you put your application in for residence? I think they're usually first-come, first-served.

LENNA: My application? What application?

SAM: Yeah, your application for residence. It's separate from your college app.

LENNA: Oh my god.

SAM: You did apply, right?

LENNA: . . . they're two separate things?

Beat.

How was I supposed to know they're two separate things?!

SAM: Give them a call. They probably still have room. There's still time.

LENNA: Yeah. Maybe.

She shifts into overdrive.

Shit. I'm such an idiot. What if they're fully booked? Apartments off campus gotta be expensive . . . and how would I even find anything so close to school starting? Here I've been buying storage totes and packing things up . . . for what?

SAM: Maybe you could see if there's any supports in place for Indigenous students? They've gotta have some kind of centre. UWin does.

LENNA: Yeah. They probably do. Or. Like.

Pause.

I guess I'm not going.

SAM: Well hold on—

LENNA: I've been stressed about leaving my dad and brother anyway. It just . . . it's not a good time. Maybe I can still defer my acceptance or whatever.

SAM: Lenna, let's just think through this for a second.

LENNA: I . . . um. I've gotta go figure this stuff out. You don't need to be worrying about this. I got it.

She stands up.

SAM: Oh. Yeah. Of course.

He stands up too.

LENNA: But uh, thanks for . . . yeah.

SAM: Of course. Anytime. Hey . . . are you okay?

LENNA: I'm . . . yep. I gotta go.

She leaves, considers going home for a second, and then walks down the road.

SCENE 11

LENNA walks deep in thought, super overwhelmed, and then lets out a frustrated sigh. Big "weight of the world on my shoulders" energy.

We hear bushes rustling and out pops JAY. He's covered in dirt and grass stains.

JAY: Howdy.

LENNA: What the heck? Jay? Where'd you come from?

JAY: *(chin pointing)* Over der. Thought I heard a ruckus so I came over to investigate.

LENNA: . . . what are you doing in the bush?

JAY: Lookin' for sweetgrass.

LENNA: Since when have you picked sweetgrass?

JAY: Since Alpha told me how much his cousin makes selling it.

LENNA: Hmm. Any luck?

JAY: Not yet. But I can smell it, so I'm getting close.
What you doin'? Ferret Butler's day off?

LENNA: What?

JAY: Ferry Wheeler's day off?

LENNA: Huh?

JAY: Fearless Leader's day off?

LENNA: Holy shit Jay, can you not?

JAY: You skipping out on something?

LENNA: No. Just getting my steps in.

JAY: Not even. Where you coming from?

LENNA: I was over at KC's.

JAY: How's Sammy doing? Wink wink!

LENNA: Oh my god, you and Dad need to chill. "How's Sam? Where's Sam? Invite Sam over for dinner! What's Sam up to?!" Not everything is about Sam!

JAY: How's Lenna doing?

LENNA: *(sighing)* Looks like I'll be sticking around a bit longer. Maybe forever. Probably forever.

JAY: What are you talking about?

LENNA: I don't have a place to stay for school. I messed up. So I might as well stay here and forget about the whole thing.

JAY: Just like that, eh.

LENNA: Just like that.

JAY: The dream is over.

LENNA: Before it even began.

JAY: Holy, all dramatic.

LENNA: I learned from the best.

JAY dusts himself off a little and sits on the ground. He gestures to LENNA to join him.

JAY: I guess Dad was right then, eh?

LENNA: Right about what?

JAY: KC told me that he was buttering up Sam, trying to get him to feel more welcome. He figured if you had someone else to stick around for, you'd drop school and stay home. So . . . he was right.

LENNA: What? No.

JAY: Guy doesn't want you to leave.

LENNA: Why'd she tell you, and not me?

JAY: Didn't see a point. She said you always seemed pretty set on leaving.

LENNA: I still want to go.

They sit in silence.

JAY: How much do you need to find an apartment?

LENNA looks at him.

I think I can give you enough for first and last, but you'll have to figure the rest out. Get a job flippin' burgs or something.

LENNA: I'm not taking your money.
Wait, why do you have money?

JAY: I've been saving. Never know when something might come up. I make decent money at the farm. And Dad doesn't charge rent.

LENNA: And you drink his pop.

JAY: Oh yeah. Still owe him one.

The wind blows and the smell of sweetgrass fills the air. They both take a big sniff.

LENNA: You're right, it is somewhere around here. The sweetgrass.

Shift.

I worry about you and Dad, you know. I keep thinking the second I leave, you're gonna kill each other. Or you'll never talk to each other ever again.

JAY: You don't gotta worry about us.

LENNA: But I do.
You guys were close when we were younger, I remember. There's pictures somewhere to prove it. We used to do stuff together, like go out in the boat all day, fishing and swimming. We all had fun, then one day you stopped coming with us. What happened to that?

JAY: You don't remember?

LENNA shakes her head.

JAY: It started after Mom left . . . Dad started blaming me for all the shit that went wrong. It was like . . . a switch went off or something. Got worse when he got sick. Or maybe it was because he was sick, I dunno. I tried to help him in the beginning, but everything I did just pissed him off.

Are you sure you don't remember any of this? One day the two of us went to the store, we were out of eggs. I was like fourteen. He says, "I'll stay in the truck." So I go in, get the eggs, then I remember how you've been begging us to have s'mores so I pick up some marshmallows, chocolate, and graham crackers. I'm standing at the cash when I start to hear this truck horn blaring outside. Must've thought I was taking too long. So I try to hurry up and I throw everything in the bag and it isn't till I get outside that I remember . . . eggs. Sure enough I look down and they're smashed to shit. Everything in the bag was coated. I look over at the truck and I meet Dad's eyes, and somehow he knows. He gets out, rips the bag out of my hand, and throws it on the ground. Screams at me about how I'm irresponsible, no good. So . . . that was it. I say I'm done, I'm out. And I start walking.

"Where the hell do you think you're goin?" he yells. I don't answer him. And he takes off. Drives right past me.

I couldn't even say half the shit I wanted to say to him. I couldn't tell him, "Calm down, I'm only fourteen," because that didn't mean anything to him. So I kept walking. Thinking about all the things I wished I said. Over and over. I finally made it back to the rez and headed into the bush, not really thinking about where I was going. Too mad. Eventually I came up to this trailer. Seemed abandoned, quiet. Ended up staying there for three days. Who lets their kid just take off like that without looking for them?

When I heard a truck pull up outside, I thought for a second it might be Dad. Then I took a look—and there was KC.

She told me to get in the truck so I did, and we drove back to her house. I stayed there for a few more days before she took me back home. When I walked in the house, Dad didn't say anything. Not a word. And that's kinda how it's been ever since. And that day, that's when I realized he didn't care about me so I figured, why should I? Started smoking that summer. Other shit followed, and . . . that's why you didn't get your s'mores.

LENNA: You never talked to him about it?

JAY: I'm no Dr. Phil.

LENNA: And that's why you and Dad always seem like you're walking on . . . eggshells.

JAY: There it is.

LENNA: No but seriously.

JAY: I don't really hold it against him anymore. Mom leaving messed him up and then he almost died because of his heart thing. I get it.

LENNA: You should talk to him. Try, at least.

JAY: Someday.

LENNA: I remember you not coming home with him that day.
He said you were staying over at a friend's. I didn't even know anything was wrong.
I'm sorry.

JAY: You were just a kid.

LENNA: So were you.

JAY: Anyway, all that to say it's okay for you to leave. We'll be fine.

LENNA: Are you sure it's okay to borrow your money?

JAY: That's what family's for.

LENNA: For money?

JAY: Ehhh, get outta here. You're ruining the moment.

LENNA: I'll pay you back. I promise. I'll get a job. And I'll look for bursaries and stuff.

JAY: Don't know what that is, but I believe ya.
Shh. Hold on a second.

JAY walks off, sniffing the air. He comes back a few moments later with a couple strands of sweetgrass.

LENNA: You found some!

JAY: Told ya it was here. You better take off, Lenna. Don't wanna attract any competition.

LENNA: Fine. Are you gonna be home later?

JAY: Nah, party at Wiley's.

LENNA: Okay. I'm gonna head back to the house.
And hey . . . thanks.

She hugs him. He returns it, takes a big whiff of the sweetgrass in his hand, then holds it out for LENNA.

JAY: To new beginnings.

LENNA takes the sweetgrass. JAY heads back into the bush.

SCENE 12

A few days pass. The wind shifts. LENNA *sits outside her house with* KC, *drinking sun tea.*

KC: That's great, my girl. When can you move in?

LENNA: Anytime between now and the end of August. They said they'll hold it for me. I can't believe it.

So depending on your schedule, we can head up whenever. I've got gas money, and maybe we can find a restaurant or something when we get there.

KC: I wanna get you some groceries too, get you going. You can start surviving on microwave popcorn the week after classes start.

LENNA: Yeah. That sounds good, thanks.

KC: The first Little to go to college! Woohoo! I'm so excited for you. You've worked real hard for this, and I know you're gonna love it.

LENNA: Uh hey, how's Sam doing?

KC *elbows* LENNA *jokingly.*

KC: Ohh, he's been asking about you too. He hides it well, but he's been a li'l hound dog. Did something happen between you two?

LENNA: I messed things up a bit. Freaked out a little.

KC: Don't think that's the case, not with the way he's been trying to check up on you. Seems like he just wants to make sure you're okay. Now, I'm not telling you what to do, but maybe you should go see him. I dunno.

KC gets up and starts heading back to her place.

LENNA: . . . umm, hey, could you tell him to come outside?

KC: Yeah. Will do. Baamaapii.

KC goes into her house. A few moments later, SAM pops his head out.

SAM: Hey, hi! KC said you wanted to see me?

LENNA: Yeah. C'mon. Let's go.

SAM: What?

LENNA: Let's go for a ride.

Shift. LENNA drives them out to the bush. She parks and they walk together to a small clearing. The sky is a cacophony of colours.

Soundscape: crickets, frogs, birds, water running through a small creek nearby. Wind in trees.

LENNA leads the way, SAM a few steps behind.

LENNA: My misho gave me this land when he passed a few years ago.

SAM: This is it. This is the place I saw. It's yours? Like you own it?

LENNA: Sort of. Like, legally it's under my name. But you can't really own land . . . anyway . . . yeah. We can go sit over there.

She sprays some mosquito repellent then tosses it in SAM's direction. He spritzes a bit on him and in the air around him then hands it back. LENNA puts the bottle back in her pocket.

They walk toward a pile of tree stumps and sit, taking in the sounds and smells around them.

My misho used to bring me out here to hunt and fish. But there hasn't been much out here other than mosquitoes since he died. It's like the animals know he's gone, somehow. Like they're respecting his space and staying away. So now I kinda just hang out. I don't wanna let it get overgrown with weeds, so I come out here when I can.

SAM: Like your misho is using the force from the grave.

He makes a "force field" buzzing sound.

LENNA: Wow. Big nerd reference there.

He laughs and lightly leans into her side, testing the waters.

SAM: What do you think it means? That I saw this place in my head before.

LENNA: I dunno. Are you spiritual? Or traditional?

SAM: Not really. You?

LENNA: Depends on the day.

A heron flies over them. They watch.

So my dad came up with this idea to try to get me to stay home. He thought if you and him became buddies, you'd stick around, and in turn so would I.

SAM: Why would you stay if I did?

LENNA: I don't really have friends around here anymore; they all left for school and haven't come back. We all went our separate ways, slowly stopped talking.

SAM: Same thing happened with some of my friends. It sucks.

LENNA: Yeah. I mean he's not wrong, I don't wanna leave everything I know behind, but I just . . . can't stop thinking about what's out there.

SAM: Like my dream.

LENNA: Yeah. Jay is helping me cover first and last for an apartment. It's not the best place, but it's close to the school, and I guess it's mostly students that live there anyway so . . . should be interesting.

SAM: That's incredible. I'm really glad that all worked out.

LENNA: Me too.

SAM: So you'll be leaving soon.

LENNA: Yeah, a couple days probably. I told KC we can go whenever.

SAM: I thought . . . never mind. It's dumb.

LENNA: What?

SAM: I guess I started to wonder about us hanging out more.

LENNA: "Hanging out."

SAM: Yeah, getting to know each other better.

Neither of them can look at each other.

LENNA: I mean . . . we can still hang out. We're hanging out right now.

SAM: Yeah. And hey. Thanks for bringing me out here.

LENNA: I needed to bring someone. And you seem trustworthy enough. Maybe between the two of us, we can both take care of this place? Make sure it doesn't get too weedy?

SAM: Absolutely. I'd love to.

LENNA: Thank you. I mean, miigwetch.

SAM: Is there a word for "you're welcome"?

LENNA: I'm not sure.

They breathe together, and then SAM *gently lifts* LENNA*'s chin up toward him. They lean in.*

SCENE 13

The Little house. It's late. There's a squeaky fan oscillating by the table. DAD *comes in from down the hall, puts the kettle on, and goes to sit in the living room. He reads the paper.*

LENNA *heads toward the house and walks in.*

DAD: Howdy.

LENNA: Hey. You're up late.

DAD: Couldn't sleep.
How was your evening?

LENNA: It was fine.

DAD: You hear from Jay today?

LENNA: Yeah, saw him earlier. He said he was going to a friend's place tonight.

DAD: Huh.

Beat.

So where were you?

LENNA: Went out with Sam.

DAD: Ohhh yeah?

LENNA: Yeah. Oh, and I heard about your little plan.

DAD: Which one?

LENNA: The one with Sam.

DAD: Oh. Well did it work?

LENNA: No.

DAD goes back to reading the paper.

So we can't even talk about it?

DAD: What's there to talk about? You're leaving. That's it.

LENNA: It's not like I'm never coming back.

He doesn't respond.

I just . . . wish you could be happy for me.

DAD: *(finally looking at her)* You don't think I'm happy for you?

LENNA: Doesn't seem like it. No.

DAD: I am.

LENNA: Then why haven't you said anything?

Beat.

Dad.

He gets up.

DAD: Well, gotta get to the store early in the morning.

He starts to head down the hall, ending the conversation.

LENNA: Jay told me about the time he ran away.

He stops.

DAD: Did he now.

LENNA: Yeah. And how you didn't try to find him. And you know what? I think that was a pretty shitty thing to do.

DAD: You do.

LENNA: I do. Were you just gonna let him fend for himself out there?

DAD: You think you've got it all figured out, huh? Worst dad ever? Where's my trophy?

She doesn't answer.

Turn off the lights when you're done out here. And make sure the door's locked. If Jay's gonna be out this late, he sure as hell ain't coming back to wake me up in the middle of the night.

LENNA: You can't keep doing this.

DAD: Doing what?

LENNA: The guilt trips! The disrespect toward me, toward Jay. We're done with that. Neither of us are kids anymore. And even if we were . . . it's not okay. And while we're at it, I'm sick of you bossing me around, getting me to do everything around here. I am not your caretaker. I'm not your nurse. I'm not your maid. I'm sick of you treating Jay like shit, he doesn't deserve it. And neither do I! I mean, is this what it was like for mom? Huh? Is this why she left? She was fed up? I get it! I'm fed up too. Yeah. And. Y'know what? Maybe . . . maybe this is exactly why I need to get out of here . . . maybe I'll finally be able to breathe for once . . . I—I won't come back . . . you . . . hear me?

. . . Well? Aren't you gonna say something?

He goes and sits on the edge of the couch.

DAD: It was . . . pretty hard when your mom left us. I didn't know how . . . how to really raise two kids on my own. Even when your mom and I were together, neither of us knew much about anything. We weren't ready to start a family. Your mom always dreamed of going off into the world, travelling, trying new things. She never wanted this life. She didn't want to stay here. She knew this place already, had it figured out. Knew its limitations. And then she got pregnant . . . so she stayed, cuz it was the right thing to do. I tried to be there for her, as much as I could. And she tried to be okay with her choice, but it started to eat away at her. She started to resent things. Me, mostly. I wanted you two to have a mom so bad, I—I think I pushed her too far. I held her too tight. So she ran.
And that day when Jay left . . . I don't know.
I guess I wanted to try a different approach. But that didn't work out too well either.
I—I can't win, Lenna.
No matter what I do, everybody leaves.
But I'm . . . trying.

LENNA: You're trying.

DAD: I care about you and your brother deeply. I'm just not always sure how to show it. Man.
Your misho wasn't as good to me as he was to you. It's like something changed in him, y'know, when you were born. He learned how to be a good grandpa.

LENNA: . . . I—uh, I started having this dream a while ago. It comes and goes. Just when I think it's gone and I'm not gonna dream about it anymore, it comes back. It's like it knows when I start to forget, or get off track. It sounds dumb, but in the dream I'm a bird. And I'm excited about exploring the world through my bird eyes. So I do. I start to fly away from everything I know, everyone I've met. And I feel really good, exploring the unknown. I feel strong. But that feeling never lasts long. I fall from the sky and suddenly everything is on fire, and the world around me is unfamiliar and dangerous. Then I feel this little tug on my foot, and I look down to see this chain wrapped around my ankle. The fire starts to close in on me and then I hear this voice calling for me somewhere in the distance. So I go to it, and it leads me to our backyard. And I keep following the chain on my ankle to this cage, while the voice encourages me that everything is okay, and that I'm safe now. I step inside, and it's uncomfortable. The cage is too small. I feel too squished. But the door slams shut. Then I wake up.

DAD: What kinda bird are you?

LENNA: Does that matter?

DAD: It might. Sometimes things visit us in our dreams because we're more willing to listen to them that way. Most of the time when we dream, we accept what we see and go along with it.

Beat.

Do you remember when your mom and Misho used to call you Bineshiinh?

LENNA: No . . . what's that mean?

DAD: Bird. Never knew why they called you that, never asked. I figured it was because you liked that big yellow bird on TV.

LENNA: Big Bird.

DAD: Yeah, he was.
I think you started getting confused about your real name. So they stopped.

Beat.

I hope you know that all I've ever wanted to do is keep you safe. And I always thought that meant making sure you stayed here with me. But I . . . I can see it now. Staying here is hurting you. You need to get out and spread your wings, see where they take you. Most of the world is shit but there's gotta be some good stuff out there somewhere.

LENNA: This is always going to be home to me.

DAD: I know.

JAY walks in.

JAY: Evenin'.

LENNA: You're home early.

JAY: Yeah . . . boss called and asked if I could come in for a shift in the morning. Said I'd do it.

DAD: Huh.

JAY: Yeah.

LENNA: How was the party?

JAY: Wiley's uncle wrecked it. Drank all the beer and kicked everybody out.

DAD: He used to do that back in the day too.

LENNA: I'm gonna go get ready for bed. Goodnight.

JAY: Night.

LENNA heads down the hall.

DAD: You heading to bed too?

JAY: I might stay up for a bit.

DAD: You want some tea?

JAY: Sure.

DAD: We're outta milk though, so you'll have to drink it plain.

DAD preps the mugs, tossing a Red Rose tea bag in each.

JAY: We're getting busier at the farm, won't have much free time for a bit. They actually said they're considering me for a better position. More hours.

DAD: You ready for that?

JAY: We'll have to see.

DAD fills the teakettle with water and turns it on.

SCENE 13A

The stage clears and radio sounds re-emerge. Static. Birds. Static. Wind. Static. Water. Then a song. A bird sings.

LENNA: *(in Ojibwe)* It's good to see you.

BIRD: *(in Ojibwe)* It's good to be seen.

LENNA: *(in Ojibwe)* I'm leaving soon.

BIRD: *(in Ojibwe)* That's okay. We'll see each other again.

The BIRD *flies away.*

SCENE 14

KC's house.

KC: So we're driving back to my place—

LENNA: To your place?? KC!

KC: Oh calm down. We took his car, he was just dropping me off. So anyway, we're driving and when we get to the rez, he slows down. Like, way down. I look around thinking, "Oh maybe there's a cop around," but nope, I don't see anybody. I keep waiting for him to say something but he doesn't, he just keeps going on, talking about whatever so finally I go, "Hey . . . is everything okay?" and he says, "Yeah, why?" and I say, "Uh . . . because I think I've walked home faster than you're driving." He's quiet for a moment, doesn't say anything. Then he points out something on the side of the road and says, "What about that?"

. . . it was a speed-limit sign. It says forty kilometres per hour. I bust out laughing and I'm like, "You think we pay attention to that?" Holy smokes. That was the cutest thing I've seen in a while.

LENNA: So when are you seeing him again?

KC: If you must know, we're supposed to hit up that farmers' market in town together next week.

LENNA: Awe!!!

KC: *(smiling)* Whatever.

KC heads into the kitchen.

SAM: KC's been singing Shania Twain songs all morning.

LENNA: Shania's her go-to when she's in a good mood.

SAM: My mom's too. Must be a sister thing.

LENNA: Definitely.

SAM: I've been doing some thinking, and I've decided I'm gonna stay here for a while.
I need some more time to figure out what I wanna do. Maybe I'll go back to school. Maybe not. Maybe I'll try to reach out to my dad, or my cousins . . . maybe not.

Beat.

Maybe I'll go fishing with your dad.

LENNA playfully shoves him.

LENNA: Maybe you could come up and see me sometime?

SAM: Definitely.

LENNA: Did you tell KC you're staying?

SAM: No, not yet.

KC: *(off stage)* Tell KC what?

She re-emerges.

SAM: I wanna stay here for a while. Is that okay?

KC: Of course. I told you you're always welcome here, Sam.

KC pulls them in for a side hug.

(to LENNA) You too, my girl.

She gives them both a big squeeze.

The lights shift, and the stage now looks like a sunset. DAD *and* JAY *enter and everyone stands, watching the sun go down. After a few moments it turns into night, and fireflies light up the sky.*

Blackout.

End of play.

ACKNOWLEDGEMENTS

Miigwetch (thank you) to the Ontario Arts Council, Native Earth Performing Arts, Aluna Theatre, Blyth Festival, Paprika Festival, and the Banff Centre for Arts and Creativity for supporting the development of *Niizh*. Miigwetch to all that have been part of *Niizh*'s journey and who continue to support mine as a storyteller.

Special chi-miigwetches to: Falen Johnson, Keith Barker, Isaac Thomas, Tara Beagan, Jeff Ho, Ali Joy Richardson, Lindsay Lachance, Theresa Cutknife, Christopher Mejaki, Jesse Wabegijig, Michaela Washburn, JD Smith, Nicole Joy Fraser, Mitchell Saddleback, Taran Kootenhayoo, Chanin Payea, Jonathan Fisher, Merewyn Comeau, Braiden Houle, Reneltta Arluk, Kevin Loring, Deneh'Cho Thompson, Jessica Campbell-Maracle, Jenna Geen, Aren Okemaysim, Vance Banzo, Cherish Violet Blood, and desirée leverenz.

Joelle Peters is an award-winning Anishinaabekwe actor/playwright working in theatre, television, and film and current Artistic Director of Native Earth Performing Arts. Her plays include *Niizh*, *Frozen River (nîkwatin sîpiy)* (co-written with Michaela Washburn and Carrie Costello), and *do you remember?* Joelle has performed at theatres and festivals across the country, including the Stratford Festival, SummerWorks, the Thousand Islands Playhouse, Western Canada Theatre, and more. She can be seen in the hit TV show *Shoresy* (Crave/Hulu), the film *In Her City* (Raven West Films Ltd.), and *Web of Lies* (Discovery+). Joelle has also narrated three audiobooks with Penguin Random House Canada. In 2020, Joelle was selected as the playwriting protegé for the Siminovitch Prize by laureate Tara Beagan. In 2021, *Frozen River (nîkwatin sîpiy)* was awarded the Sharon Enkin Plays for Young People Award at the annual Tom Hendry Awards. In 2023, the premiere production of *Niizh* was nominated for four Dora Mavor Moore Awards. Keep up with Joelle at joellepeters.ca and on Instagram: @joellepeters.jpg.